Teach Your Child To Swim: Breaststroke Bootcamp

Written by AlyT

Teach Your Child To Swim: Breaststroke Bootcamp
Part of the Teach Your Child To Swim series
with AlyT

DEDICATED TO

my mother **RHONDA** aka **MRS PAUL**
who taught me everything I needed to know about life †
AND my mentor **MR TIBBS** aka **TIBBSIE** ; both of whom helped mould me into the swimmer and swimming teacher I am today.

Written by AlyT

© Copyright 2024 by Allison Tyson. All rights reserved.

First printing: July, 2024

Disclaimer
While we draw on our professional expertise and background in teaching learn to swim and swimming training, by purchasing and reading our products you acknowledge that we have produced this book for informational and educational purposes only. You alone are solely responsible and take full responsibility for your own wellbeing as well as the health, lives and well-being of your family and children in your care in and around water.

Stay in touch:
Born to Swim, P.O Box 6699, Cairns City, QLD 4870
SwimMechanics@yahoo.com
www.BornToSwim.com.au
www.PoweredByChlorine.com
Instagram @LearnToSwimTheAustralianWay
Etsy Store www.borntoswimglobal.etsy.com
Most titles available from Etsy, Amazon and all good online Book Retailers

Other titles by this Author:
Water Awareness Newborns
Water Awareness Babies
Water Awareness Toddlers
Learn to Swim the Australian Way Level 1 The Foundations
Learn to Swim the Australian Way Level 2 The Basics
Learn to Swim the Australian Way Level 3 Intermediate
Learn to Swim the Australian Way Level 4 Advanced
The Ultimate Pool Party Planner
Focus On Freestyle: Teaching Guide
Water Safety: Teaching Guide
Breaststroke Bootcamp: Teaching Guide
Butterfly Bootcamp: Teaching Guide
Backstroke Bootcamp: Teaching Guide
Learning To Float: Color Me In & Learn To Swim Activity Book
A Float For Every Stroke: Teaching Body Position
Visual Aids For Inclusive Aquatic Education: 100+ Swimming Flashcards
Welcome To Swim Squad: Activity Book For Swimmers
Welcome To Water Safety: Activity Book For Swimmers
Eat Pray Swim: A Swimmer's Logbook & Prayer Journal
Thalassophile: Logbook & Journal For Lovers Of The Ocean and Sea
Competitive Swimming Quotes: Coloring Book For Adults & Teens
Wild Swimming Quotes: Coloring Book For Adults & Teens
Mermaids: Coloring Book For Adults & Teens
Powered By Chlorine : Logbooks & Journals For Swimmers

A NOTE TO ALL THE BUDDING BREASTSTROKERS!!

Welcome to Born To Swim's BREASTSTROKE BOOTCAMP!!

So, you want to build a BETTER BREASTSTROKE, right?

Well we've put together a whole bunch of skills from our LEARN TO SWIM THE AUSTRALIAN WAY series plus+ some additional DRILLS FOR SKILLS, designed to take Breaststroke to the NEXT LEVEL, or maybe just put it back on the right track.

We know that when it comes to Breaststroke it's a COMPLICATED STROKE and can be a bit tricky; whether you're learning it or teaching it.

Pulling too wide, a wonky kick, a mis-timed breath or even getting lost in a vortex?! Breaststroke can literally make or break an I.M (Individual Medley) and easily get a swimmer D.Q'd (disqualified) if not performed correctly!!

But hey, we've got the SOLUTION!

In this guide we've BROKEN DOWN EACH COMPONENT of Breaststroke, one skill at a time, to fast track swimmers to a BETTER BREASTSTROKE.

Best of luck with besting your Breaststroke,

Aly T

SAFETY FIRST!

⚠️ Never swim alone

⚠️ Always keep children within arms reach

⚠️ Remove distractions when teaching in water

⚠️ Never force a swimmer under the water

⚠️ Do not play breath holding games or encourage holding the breath for long periods of time

✓ Learning to swim in shallow, waist depth water is best for beginners

✓ Learning CPR & First Aid Saves Lives

FLEXIBILITY TRAINING

TIP: Flexible but strong ankles, hips & knees are an absolute must for better Breaststroke

Why do it?
Unlike the other three competitive strokes, Breaststroke requires an outward flexing of the feet for correct leg propulsion. Tight ankles & limited hip or knee rotation can lead to failing to 'turn the feet out' resulting in a DQ for an 'illegal wonky kick' or limited propulsion.

Frog Feet Pose

Flexible knees, ankles & hips allow breaststrokers to achieve a greater range of motion & generate more propulsive power during the kick

Chair Leg Curls

Penguin Stance

How to do it?
To improve muscle memory & ankle flexibility and to encourage the correct outward flexing of the feet BEFORE teaching the kick try these:
- Chair Leg Curls - curling the feet around the legs of a chair, keeping the knees together, to loosen tight ankles and turning the knees inward
- The Penguin Stance/Walk - heels together with feet turned outward in a V
- Frog Feet 'V' Pose - sitting or laying in the water with feet turned out & heels together in a 'V'

FOOT PROPULSION

Why do it?

Vertical balancing on a pool noodle teaches swimmers to move through the water and spin by toying with the angle of their feet & rotation of their knees. Unlike the other competitive strokes, Breaststroke kick relies upon the angular tilt of the feet to 'catch the water' with a circular trajectory of the knees rather than the usual up and down motion of the Butterfly, Backstroke and Freestyle kick.

TIP

Use vertical balancing or treading water to 'warm-up' the feet, ankles & hips

find traction with your feet

How to do it?

1. Climb onto a pool noodle like you are climbing onto a horse
2. Stay upright by holding onto the the neck of the noodle with both hands
3. Do not lean too far forward or backward, otherwise you'll become unbalanced
4. Use only your feet & legs to spin and turn in a slow circle
5. Practise changing direction and moving forward using only your feet and legs
6. Try it without the noodle and tread water using the 'Egg Beater Kick'

MISSILE FROG FLOAT

How to do it?
1. Stretch out flat in shallow water and extend the arms forward to hold onto a submerged step or bottom of the pool
2. Stretch your legs out behind you with feet apart
3. Squeeze your elbows against the side of your head and look straight down
4. Bend your knees and draw your feet up BEHIND you
5. Turn your feet out and bring your heels together
6. Relax, balance and Frog Float in this position

Frog Float

Missile Glide

Once you can balance in this position, move to deeper water to
Missile Frog Float
1. Frog Float and bring your hands together so your thumbs are touching in the Missile Glide position
2. Squeeze your elbows against the side of your head and angle your hands with thumbs down
3. Keep the hands just below the surface & feet flat and pointing outward
5. Relax and float in this position

TIP
The arms & hands should make the shape of a 'V' and be fully extended sitting just under the surface of the water

The Missile Glide also known as the BREASTSTROKE GLIDE, resembles the Torpedo Streamline (where the hands are clasped on top of each other), but with a slight variation; the hands are positioned side-by-side, with thumbs touching, and hands facing outward.
To practise the Missile Glide:
Lay on the pool deck with arms straight & extended, thumbs touching and hands angled downward. Legs should be straight with feet together & big toes touching

Why do it?
Body positioning is crucial to swimming Breaststroke correctly to minimise excess drag or resistance from the water.
The Missile Frog Float puts the swimmer in the ideal starter body position for building the stroke: arms extended with hands & feet ready to 'catch the water'

thumbs together
heels together
Missile Frog Float

3

DRYLAND BREASTSTROKE KICK

TIP: Breaking down complex skills into a sequence of simple body positions streamlines the learning process

Why do it? Dryland practise gives the swimmer a chance to learn the correct motor skills & direction of the legs for the different phases of the Breaststroke kick.

missile — frog — starfish — missile

How to do it?
Lay on the pool deck and move through each of the following float positions:
Position 1 Missile Glide - arms extended, thumbs touching & hands angled inward, legs straight with feet together and big toes touching
Position 2 Missile Frog Float - knees bent behind you with feet turned out and heels together
Position 3 Starfish Legs - legs straight with feet apart and toes pointed
Position 4 Missile Glide - return to the starting Missile Glide position, making sure the big toes touch and legs are straight before re-starting the sequence

BREASTSTROKE FLOAT SEQUENCE

Learn the the kick sequence BEFORE adding propulsion

Why do it?
Float sequences help improve stability & balance as the swimmer transitions through the different phases of the kick as float positions. They'll also reinforce the correct muscle memory, before adding propulsion.

TIP
Work on 'narrowing the knees' AFTER perfecting the correct flexing & direction of the feet

- turn the feet out — **Bent legs**
- heels & knees rotate around — **Legs apart**
- feet together — **Legs straight**

How to do it?
After rehearsing the Breaststroke kick sequence on the pool deck, practise each position in the water as a sequence of floats

Missile Glide Float - Missile Frog Float - Starfish Legs - Missile Glide Float

Return to the starting Missile Glide position each time by snapping the legs and feet together, making sure the big toes touch as you stretch out long and count 1... 2... before re-starting the sequence

BREASTSTROKE KICKING

Don't 'relax' during the glide, keep the body taut & stretch out long & flat

find the line & glide

fast feet

look for symmetry

prioritise turning the feet out

Use 'wall kicks' to work on speed and to refine & strengthen your kick

Why do it?

Breaststroke Kicking isolates the kick so swimmers can focus on propulsion, coordination & timing whilst maintaining the correct body position.

How to do it?

1. Push off from the wall in a Missile Glide
2. Draw the feet up BEHIND you, turning them out, and swinging them around and together again until your big toes touch
3. As the feet swing around, use the soles of your feet to PUSH against the water and squeeze your legs together as you point your toes
4. Before restarting the kick, pause and count to 2 as you extend your legs and lift your heels so your feet are in line and hidden behind your body as you glide

KICKING ON THE BACK

TIP: Hold a kickboard over the knees to encourage correct body positioning

work toward narrowing the knees

Rotate the legs back & around

lengthen & glide

Why do it?

To promote body position awareness, kicking on the back encourages breaststrokers to concentrate on keeping their hips high, maintaining a streamlined body position and coordinating the rhythm of the kick. It is also useful in identifying errors and streamlining the kick

Simple Ways To Refine The Kick

- Try a kickboard over the knees to help lift the hips & stop knees from popping out of the water
- Try holding the hands behind the back to touch the heels to help swimmers learn to bring the legs straight up behind them & keep the knees closer together
- Try placing hands on the knees to help swimmers learn to rotate the knees as they turn their feet out and keep the knees closer together
- Try starting each kick with feet & legs together to help narrow the kick

How to do it?

1. Float on your back and bend your knees to draw the heels up & together BEHIND you
2. Turn your feet out so the legs are in the Frog Float pose
3. Turn your knees inward and push your feet outward
4. As the feet swing around, PUSH the water with the edge of your feet, and start to straighten your legs & point your toes
5. Snap your legs together and lift them to just below the surface
6. Hold the glide for a count of 2 before starting the next kick

DRYLAND BREASTSTROKE ARM SEQUENCE

part the water | **catch the water** | **redirect the hands** | **send the energy forward**

Why do it?
Dryland practise gives the swimmer a chance to learn & mimic complex motor skills plus refine their technique by focusing on specific aspects of the Breaststroke arm movements

TIP
Move from slow to fast, like winding up a crank, when practising the Breaststroke arms

How to do it?
1. Lay down with only your head, shoulders & arms over the side of the pool
2. Start with your face looking down into the water with your arms slightly wider than shoulder-width apart
3. Your palms should be facing out with thumbs turned downward
4. Bend your arms and push the water toward your chest as you lift up, out of the water
5. As the hands approach your chest, lift up and straighten your back so you can take in a breath
6. During the breath, redirect your hands forward into a prayer-like position so your thumbs are up and fingertips facing forward ready to shoot and extend
7. To 'Shoot', send your arms forward, up and over the water
8. To fully extend forward, press your armpits into the water and flatten the hands, palms down into the Missile Glide position, whilst pressing your face back into the water

Y-EAT-PRAY-SLIDE & GLIDE

Why do it?

Isolating & practicing breaststroke arm movements in water, allows swimmers to focus specifically on the arm technique, WITH the resistance of water, but without the distraction of coordinating other aspects of the stroke. This focused practice can help refine & perfect the arm movements before adding the kick

!! Use a pool noodle to stop the arms from sweeping too wide or pulling back too far

TIP Crunching the elbows to the ribs helps get the arms out of the way so they can slide forward with less resistance

Y • eat • pray • slide & glide

How to do it?

1. Stand in shoulder depth water or lean over a lane rope or pool noodle with your arms and face in the Missile Glide position
2. Keep looking down as you press the arms outward with the palms of your hands until they are in a 'Y' position
3. Bend the arms at the elbow so fingertips are pointing down as you 'scoop' the water toward your chest, this is the 'Eat' position
4. As you lift up for a breath, tuck and squeeze your elbows against your ribs
5. Redirect the hands forward under your chin, your thumbs should be up and hands in the 'Prayer' position ready to 'Shoot' forward
6. Slide the hands and arms forward by using the combined momentum of driving your face & torso back into the water
7. Tuck the chin and slide as far forward into the Missile Glide position before starting the next arm cycle

2 KICKS 1 PULL

Why do it?
This drill helps swimmers focus on keeping their body high in the water, stopping the swimmer from 'pulling too early' and maximising the streamline ie 'finding the line' as they extend the glide between each kick.
It also helps with timing & rhythm by separating the 'pull' from the 'kick and correct their timing'

TIP
Plunge the face forward to bring the hips up before initiating the kick

kick with arms streamlined

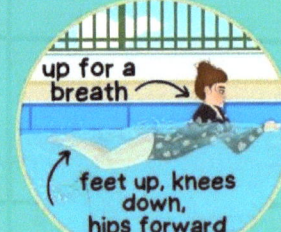
up for a breath
feet up, knees down, hips forward

find the line

pull with legs streamlined

How to do it?
1. Push off from the wall using a Missile Glide
2. Stay in the Missile Glide and do two slow Breaststroke kicks
3. As you kick, keep your face between your outstretched arms with eyes looking down at the bottom of the pool
4. Reach & extend further forward by pressing your armpits into the water.
5. After finishing the second kick, begin the Breaststroke pull by looking forward and separating the hands into the 'Y' position
6. Complete the Breaststroke arm sequence, pulling yourself up out of the water to take a breath as you 'Scoop' the forearms in and squeeze the elbows to the ribs
7. Tuck your chin and thrust your face back into the water as you 'Shoot' forward
8. Once you have flattened out into the 'Missile Glide' repeat the two kicks

Refining the Pull
You can also practise this drill
- with a 'mini pull' out front so you can work on increasing hand speed and to correct pulling too wide or pulling back too far
OR
- with a flutter kick to assist the swimmer to 'lean into the water' as they slide the arms forward into the glide

SEPARATION DRILL

Why do it?

Proper timing creates less work for the swimmer, whereas mistimed Breaststroke creates lots of resistance in the water.
To avoid 'spinning the wheels' the Separation Drill isolates the 'pull' from the 'kick'.
It helps improve body position, efficiency, timing and the streamline, for a faster, smoother Breaststroke

How to do it?
1. Start in the Missile Glide position and perform one fast kick
2. Next, perform the Breaststroke pull & recovery with your legs together & toes pointed
3. Use the pull to draw your body up & take a quick breath
4. Only after you've gone back to the Missile Glide position (streamline), do you start the next kick.
5. Practise the drill, then add some speed and slowly merge the two parts closer together

Remember to only begin the kick AFTER the hands extend forward to 'shoot'

Did You Know?
The Breastroke pull is likened to half a Butterfly pull

TIP
Each move is separate. First you pull... then you kick

get streamlined before starting the kick

fingertips down & elbows up

move the hips forward as you pull

COBRA STRIKE

Why do it?

Just like a Cobra coils and extends its body with precision and control, Breaststroke swimmers can use a similar fluid motion of contracting and expanding to propel themselves through the water.
The Cobra Strike combines speed, gravity and the whole body to give more power to Breaststroke, BUT only AFTER the kick, pull & recovery have been refined!!

How to do it?

1. Push off from the wall in the Missile Glide
2. Turn your thumbs down and press the palms against the water as you sweep outwards into the 'Y' position (outsweep)
3. Catch the water with your hands, by bending the elbows and moving your hands toward your chest, keeping the fingertips down (insweep)
4. Use the insweep to lift your head and shoulders up and out of the water
5. As you rise crunch your elbows against your ribs, getting as narrow as you can, and shrug the shoulders toward your ears (contract)
6. Arch upwards, leaning back slightly as you look forward & slightly down to take in a quick breath
7. Tuck the chin backward and use the momentum of your head driving forward to strike the water, (like a Cobra attacking it's prey)
8. Recover the hands over or just below the surface of the water and get back into the Missile Glide position (expand)
9. Missile Glide momentarily at full expansion to gather energy & focus before initiating the kick
10. Initiate a fast kick to help you lunge further forward
before beginning the next outsweep

TIP: Don't dive down too deep after each breath

- lift the torso
- laser eyes
- elbows to chest
- drive forward
- shoot forward

>>> CONTRACT <<<   <<< EXPAND >>>

OVER-UNDER DRILL

TIP
Avoid the urge to kick DOWN at the finish of the breaststroke kick, lift the heels instead

Why do it?
To utilise the undulation motion of breaststroke and focus on encouraging the coupling motion of a 'heavy head' and 'high hips' to ride over and under the bow wave by follow the natural undulating flow of the water

hips forward

Put on a pair of fins and dolphin kick with your arms out front in the Missile Glide position for 1-2-3-4 kicks.
On the 5th kick outsweep and as the hands begin the insweep, use the hands and forearms to pull water towards your chest, pulling the hips forward as your torso rises up out of the water.
As you plunge forward to strike, dolphin kick.
Don't dive TOO DEEP. It should be a fluid up and down motion each time you pull and breathe then strike forward and kick.
The dolphin kicking with fins will over-emphasize the undulation and give you the over-under sensation as you travel through the water.
Take the fins off and swim with a regular breaststroke kick to reinforce the undulation of breaststroke.
During the momentary Missile Glide the torso and arms must strike forward NOT DOWN whilst the legs must finish the kick with the lifting of the heels NOT KICKING DOWNWARD before starting the next catch.

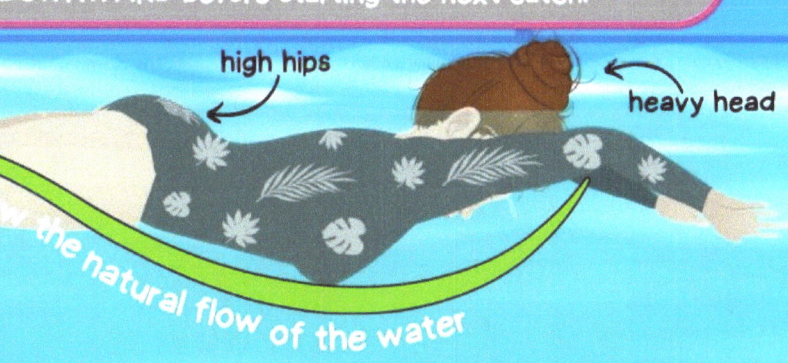

high hips

heavy head

Follow the natural flow of the water

Use Fins For This Drill

Breaststroke
LESSON PLAN

Activities Equipment: Pool Noodles, Fins & Kickboards	Activities Completed					
Flexibility Training						
Foot Propulsion						
Missile Frog Float						
Dryland Breaststroke Kick						
Breaststroke Float Sequence						
Breaststroke Kicking						
Kicking On The Back						
Dryland Breaststroke Arm Sequence						
Y - Eat - Pray - Shoot & Glide						
Two Kicks One Pull						
Separation Drill						
Cobra Strike						
Over-Under Drill						

Thank you for diving into the world of swimming with us!
We hope you've enjoyed splashing through the pages and discovering new aquatic skills.
Your feedback is invaluable to us. If you enjoyed our books, please consider leaving a review or share your experience with others. Happy swimming and thank you for being a part of our #SwimmingRevolution

www.ingramcontent.com/pod-product-compliance
Lightning Source LLC
Chambersburg PA
CBHW041526070526
44585CB00002B/103